Medically Induced Insanity

Erica Martino

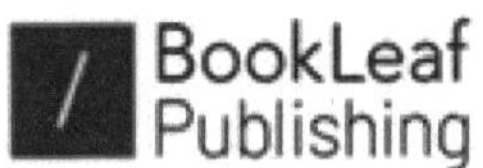

Presentation by *BookLeaf Publishing*

Web: www.bookleafpub.com

E-mail: info@bookleafpub.com

ISBN : 9789357699372

First edition 2022

DEDICATION

To all who have ever believed me, and especially those who didn't.

ALL FOR ME

I wish I'd known, but these eyes just couldn't see.
Had I only known all you'd give to me.
Butterflies, a smile, a call.
Sweet cards and flowers, I can have it all.
A friend, a lover, a ring.
Dinners, a dress, hearts connected by string.
Dogs, a baby, our little family.
So much love, you promised you'd never leave.
With all you gave, I couldn't make sense of it all.
Secrets and lies, fake truths.
Forever broken heart, a soul to follow suit.
Insecurities transformed to insanity.
Had I only known,
all you'd give to me.

WANT

I want to die.
I say it again and again,
as if ceasing would make it okay.
But it's not that I don't want life.
To the core of my being, I do.
Just maybe not this particular one...
I want away from people, or at least most of whom
I know.
Maybe I just have yet to find my tribe.
I want animals and children,
To care for, to teach, to play, to love.
Early morning coffee, late night wine.
To grow. Plants, family, myself.
Water. Still, rushing.
Forests. Mountains. Caves.
Music. Especially 'round a fire.
Stars to put me in awe.
I want to feel larger than life, and as a speck of dust.
I crave a soul crushing love, that causes no pain.
I don't want much...
just it all.

TWENTY/TWENTY

In hindsight, I should have just taken the green..
I should have taken one of your many friends up
on
their offers,
just left you behind.
I should have said goodbye at the first lie before
our union.
I should have grabbed the one thing that was
true
and ran,
tests in tow.
I shouldn't have listened as you begged all the
times I managed to go.
I should have slipped with the first recoil,
perhaps something in dinner.
I should have spoken every time asked,
even though you were always in the room.
Funny that's when it ended...

JESUS

Forgive them, for they know not what they do.
Or perhaps, maybe, they do,
but forgive them anyway.
People get fed certain lines,
and devour them as though starved.
One does tend to forget, though,
there are three sides to every story.
They know but one, ever filtered.
It will all come to light in the end.
Maybe they will soon see,
or choose to still look away...
Either way, please,
forgive them anyway.

HERO

I don't know you well, that's true.
Regardless, I love you still, no matter which side.
You may ignore me, but at one time,
you were there when needed.
Mostly I did not know til after.
You may choose not to see me, but you opened my eyes...
to the fact I could have more.
More than the mediocrity,
and that I didn't want what I'd been living.
Coincidence? Crossed stars? Backfire?
Maybe another could have done the same,
but that's a terribly big maybe.
Rough, blunt, not worried for me,
and I love you for it all.
I'm safe, at ease, nervous, and in awe.
The first time, six years later.
The next day, a year later.
Memories are scarce in the grand scheme,
yet you take up more space than most.
Even though we'll never speak again,
you're in my blood, saving me.

CAN'T LET GO

My love pushed me to you.
Again and again.
I was yours, always, I think...
I lost my mind, you dominated what was left.
And that's where I found you,
already in every part of me.
Not having you wasn't an option now.
Persistent.
Well, when I find something I need.
Someone...
Off and on.
Touch and go.
But always there, somewhere, waiting.
Little did I know, I'd gladly burn the world for you.
And just watch in awe of the explosive glory.
Many things I wish had never happened.
Lies. Betrayal. Confusion. Heartache.
Though in reality, I would do it all again.
Gladly. And more if asked.
Without all the pain, I'd never known you.
And, God, do I love how I've known you...

MACKENZIE

Even when I'm gone, I'm with you.
You'll hear me in the wind. In the rain.
Let me warm you with the sunshine.
Let yourself scream with me in the storm.
Know I am looking at you through the eyes of
our
loves...
Watching, loving. Caring, protecting.
And if you are still.
And listen so close.
You'll hear me in your heart.
Saying you belong, with each beat.

BEAUTIFUL LIES

It was never the fairy tales for me,
rather the love songs that did me in.
I don't know why,
but most people don't have the capacity,
blood or not.
By far, most encounters
are more concerned with their own heart.
No matter the words on their lips.
Learn to trust your eyes more than your ears.
Words can be beautiful,
but they are easy to hide behind,
with no follow through.
And should you happen upon one,
who does know of love...
I pray you see it,
and not hurt them... too much...
For after enough time,
they, too,
will give up on you.

CONFESSIONAL

Forgive me father,
for I have sinned...
I've given far too much.
Of my heart, my soul, away.
All in hopes of the love I've, still,
never received.
And now,
though I've tried, again and again,
I cannot seem to retrieve.
I must be doing something wrong...
Maybe I'm no longer worthy...
After much prayer and repentance,
I still can't fill the void.
And, so now, I dive in,
and hope the devil will have me.

THAT DARK NIGHT

I've always loved the words of Dylan.
So courageous and so strong.
Though, that must mean,
I am not.
I welcome that dark night,
and intend on going into it sweetly.
I've waited for so long,
it always just out of reach.
And now I summon it,
to a place it hasn't much choice.
It's the one who has been there,
always.
Since a child.
An old friend.
The only friend,
waiting to welcome me home.

ATTEMPTED MURDER

You tried to kill all the love I have inside.
And for a season, I truly thought you did.
But my heart is mine,
and she is stubborn.
She refuses to stay locked in her cage.
Rather, live life on my sleeve.
Seeing, feeling the world.
My brain tells her,
it's safer inside.
But life is meant to be felt.
And her scars, too many to number,
only show that she has.
My heart overrides my brain.
She will, now, obey my stomach,
retreating as the warnings come in.
Yet, always returning, craving adventure,
as the sirens fade.
Though I've spent countless nights,
I don't think I'll ever grasp why
you wanted to kill it...
She can be a lot. But only because she feels.
Feels at a much greater capacity than you, or
most.
Which unfortunately means the hurt is deeper...
But, by the same token, so is the joy. The love.
She is why I was always there.

Dropping anything for you.
Giving the best for all your passions.
Never mad for long. And always, always forgave.
No matter the hurt. The pain.
Believed your every word.
The part who tried everything.
To make you happy. To make it work.
No matter how it offended my soul.
You made me think I was wrong,
because of this heart I hold.
I now see
you're the one in need of help...
As you know nothing of love.
Giving or getting.
And that is sadder than our lost decades,
and thoughts of me in a ball on the floor...

NEW BEGINNINGS

Birds and bees. Flowers and trees.
And all I want is you in me.
Love is growing, life is blooming.
Look ahead, forget the looming.
Yell with the thunder
and cry with the rain.
New buds sprouting,
help forget the pain.
Dance with the wind,
free of worry and care.
It feels to me,
spring is in the air.

PEACE

All ever used for
are manly desires.
Never enough.
Not considered,
wanted,
loved.
Too much as well,
never what's required.
An escape I need,
to fly,
a dove.

HOMELESS

I'm tired of the fight.
You promised. To God.
But little good that does,
you don't even believe.
So take it all.
Turn it against me.
Just words. Yours. Mine.
Our vows, everything.
I only really wanted
for it to be you.
Now you've ruined all else,
a possible happy.
You were my arms to run to,
now they strangle.
Never wanted to be without you.
But I will survive.
I hope you do, too.

LUCIFER

Really not a secret.
All I wish you is death.
My words, hardly uttered.
Instead, being read...
So much on my face,
through my eyes and disdain.
How much have I prayed?
Ever in vain.
So much for them...
Pleads and hacksaw
attempts at curses.
Whatever. However.
Nothing. Curses.
Of course,
forever more,
still you're there.
Always waiting.
Thoughts of selling,
all of me, to the devil.
Alas, it's been done...

TUMOR

As lovely as it sounds,
you shouldn't make homes out of humans.
I know you're dying
to live in their heart.
But though, at first, you're keeping them warm...
You'll soon be a thorn.
Bothersome. Malignant.
They'll despise you, wish you gone.
And too afraid of the cut.
So, they'll try to rip you apart.
Make you leave in pieces.
Use drugs.
To shrink you, to kill you.
Will you let them?
Or take over...

CHOOSE

To be kind,
when the world is not.
To love,
with your heart breaking.
To give people chances,
even when they've made mistakes.
To open your heart,
after you've lost your soul.
To grow,
when it will get washed away.
To bleed,
though it's never reciprocated.
To build,
after all has been burned.
To sing,
when your voice is trembling.
To dance,
in the storm.

GOAT

Say what you will,
you'll never get under my skin.
And, try as you might,
your words won't hurt,
however ugly they make you.
This armor is kevlar
after what I've been through.
I don't get mad at dogs
for barking at me.
It's what they're bred to do.
I cannot make you see the lies,
blatant as they may be.
The manipulation used on you
was once used on me.
I guess this is just what happens
when you become the world's muse...

YULETIDE

Execution.
By Christmas lights.
Really,
it does sound like you...
To take something special,
that brings me joy,
that I love
and put above all else.
For you to use it against me.
But,
you know,
I've been watching, learning.
So don't underestimate,
or you may just find them
around your neck
instead of mine.

PHOENIX

Be cautious.
She may love you,
with all of her heart, soul, being.
More than herself.
But only so much can be allowed.
You can lie, cheat.
You can badmouth, gossip.
Steal and starve.
But one day,
when enough is enough,
she'll open up...
All that you want,
need, desire,
pretend to love,
will burn.
And she will rise.
Again.

REVIVAL

I've spent so long now
trying to bring back
the parts of me
you suffocated.
I was sure
my fire had been extinguished.
Yet, after blowing
and fanning for years,
I can see small embers glow again.
The parts that believe.
In love and humanity.
The trust I was sure
was gone for good.
The colors I had forgotten
that I could see.
The beauty that has always
lived in, surrounded me.

Printed by Libri Plureos GmbH in Hamburg, Germany